SU

Review & Analysis of
Weinberg and Mares' Book

Traction

BusinessNews Publishing

BOOK PRESENTATION: *TRACTION* BY GABRIEL WEINBERG AND JUSTIN MARES

SUMMARY OF *TRACTION* (GABRIEL WEINBERG AND JUSTIN MARES)

BOOK PRESENTATION: *TRACTION* BY GABRIEL WEINBERG AND JUSTIN MARES

BOOK ABSTRACT

All startups have a product. What differentiates the winners from the losers, however, is successful startups generate "traction" – real customer growth and momentum. The pursuit of traction in the marketplace should be the central aim of anyone who is trying to get a startup off the ground.

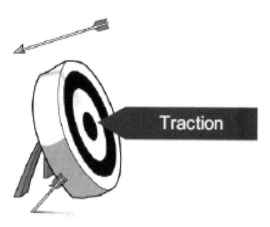

So how do you generate traction? There are at least nineteen channels which have been used successfully by other startups. It's pretty much impossible to tell in advance which of these channels will end up working for you so usually you have to road test a few and then build on what works.

A good framework for identifying which traction channels you should be using is the "Bullseye Framework" which looks like this:

1. **Brainstorm** – identify how each traction channel could work for you
2. **Rank** – compare the various traction channels using consistent criteria
3. **Prioritize** – identify the three traction channels which look most promising
4. **Test** – start using those three channels and measure what results
5. **Focus** – commit all your resources to the best-performing traction channel

ABOUT THE AUTHOR

GABRIEL WEINBERG is founder and CEO of DuckDuckGo, an online search engine which started in 2008 and delivered more than one billion searches in 2013. He is also an active angel investor. He's been featured on CBS and FOX, and written about in The Guardian and The Washington

Post. He previously co-founded and served as CEO of Opobox which was acquired in 2006. Gabriel Weinberg is a graduate of MIT.

JUSTIN MARES is former director of revenue and growth at Exceptional, a software company acquired by Rackspace in 2013. Before that, he founded two other startups, one of which went well and one of which closed down. He runs a growth meetup in San Francisco and writes on marketing in his personal blog at justinmares.com. Justin Mares is a graduate of the University of Pittsburgh.

IMPORTANT NOTE ABOUT THIS EBOOK

This is a summary and not a critique or a review of the book. It does not offer judgment or opinion on the content of the book. This summary may not be organized chapter-wise but is an overview of the main ideas, viewpoints and arguments from the book as a whole. This means that the organization of this summary is not a representation of the book.

SUMMARY OF *TRACTION* (GABRIEL WEINBERG AND JUSTIN MARES)

HOW TO THINK ABOUT TRACTION

Generating traction has to be an obsession for startups. Apply five principles:

1. Use Bullseye to start generating traction
2. Always spend 50% of your time on traction
3. Be prepared to pivot on evidence of more traction
4. Watch for channel saturation – it's coming
5. Always have a traction goal that moves the needle

1. USE BULLSEYE TO START GENERATING TRACTION

Traction is a sign that your company is taking off and will be able to find enough customers to stay in business. The whole point of a startup is you have to grow quickly. Simply put, to keep the doors open as a startup, you need to generate traction ASAP.

There are at least nineteen different channels you can use to generate traction. Companies have excelled using each and every one of them at different times. However, there will usually be just one or two which will work for you. The best way to find your traction channel is to use the Bullseye Framework:

1. **Brainstorm** – identify how each traction channel could work for you
2. **Rank** – compare the various traction channels using consistent criteria
3. **Prioritize** – identify the three traction channels which look most promising
4. **Test** – start using those three channels and measure what results
5. **Focus** – commit all your resources to the best-performing traction channel

Note you start Bullseye by visualizing how each of those nineteen channels might work out for you in practice. The criteria you then use in step 2 to narrow your choices down to the best three are:

- Which traction channels look most promising?
- How probable is it that this channel might work?
- What would be the cost to acquire a customer?
- How many customers could you reasonably expect?
- How long would it take to see success?

Once you identify your best three traction channels, you then start running some tests for each of those channels. You do this in parallel rather than sequentially so you can get answers quickly. As you run those tests, keep track of:

- How much it costs you to acquire a customer.
- How many customers that channel could generate.
- Whether the customers you get are a good fit.

Most of the time, one of the three channels you test will end up shining for you. When that happens, you then focus all your resources and efforts on optimizing that channel. You keep running experiments in that traction channel to uncover effective tactics and scale them.

> *"It is very likely that one channel is optimal. Most businesses actually get zero distribution channels to work. Poor distribution—not product—is the number one cause of failure. If you can get even a single distribution channel to work, you have great business. If you try for several but don't nail one, you're finished. So it's worth thinking really hard about finding the single best distribution channel."*
>
> *- Peter Thiel, founder, PayPal*

> *"A startup is a company designed to grow fast. Being newly founded does not in itself make a company a startup. Nor is it necessary for a startup to work on technology, or take venture funding, or have some sort of 'exit.' The only essential thing is growth. Everything else we associate with startups follows from growth."*
>
> *- Paul Graham, founder, Y Combinator*

"Research how past and present companies in your space and adjacent spaces succeeded or failed at getting traction. The easiest way to do this is to go talk to startup founders who previously failed at what you're trying to do."

- Gabriel Weinberg and Justin Mares

2. ALWAYS SPEND 50% OF YOUR TIME ON TRACTION

"The number one reason that we pass on entrepreneurs we'd otherwise like to back is their focusing on product to the exclusion of everything else. Many entrepreneurs who build great products simply don't have a good distribution strategy. Even worse is when they insist that they don't need one, or call [their] no distribution strategy a 'viral marketing strategy.'"

- Marc Andreeson, founder of Netscape and venture capital firm Andreeson-Horowitz

"If you're starting a company, chances are you can build a product. Almost every failed startup has a product. What failed startups don't have are enough customers. Many entrepreneurs think that if you build a killer product, your customers will beat a path to your door. We call this line of thinking The Product

Trap: the fallacy that the best use of your time is always improving your product. In other words, "if you build it, they will come" is wrong."

- Gabriel Weinberg and Justin Mares

Traction is so important to the survival of a startup that fully 50% of your time should be allocated to generating traction. You can spend the other half of your time working on your product. This "50% Rule" has several important advantages:

1. You'll actually end up building a better product because you will be able to incorporate knowledge from your traction efforts into your product development. Feedback from early customers will help you get more customers in the future.
2. By working on traction and product development in parallel, you will be experimenting and testing different traction channels before you launch. This gives you a head-start so when your product is ready, you can grow rapidly.
3. Bullseye is a lean approach to marketing. You run some cheap experiments and then expand what works and drop what does not.
4. Going after traction and product simultaneously increases the odds that you will develop a product for which you can actually get traction in the marketplace.

3. BE PREPARED TO PIVOT ON EVIDENCE OF MORE TRACTION

Many successful companies start out to make one product but ultimately find success doing something entirely different. In other words, they pivot. Traction is a great indicator of when a pivot is needed and whether it will succeed.

If you're considering a pivot for your startup, look for evidence of traction and/or product engagement in the direction you're thinking about heading. A lot of the future viability of your startup hinges on choosing a great market at just the right time. Traction is the perfect criteria for making that call.

> *"If you're not seeing the traction you want, look for bright spots in your user base, pockets of users that are truly engaged with your product. See if you can figure out why it works for them and if you can expand from that base. If there are no bright spots, it may be a good time to pivot."*
>
> *- Gabriel Weinberg and Justin Mares*

4. WATCH FOR CHANNEL SATURATION _ IT'S COMING

Over time, all marketing channels become saturated and lose their effectiveness. They may become too expensive, too crowded or consumers may move on to other technologies. To combat that reality, you should be running small and cheap experiments in other traction channels all the time.

If you're consistently running cheap tests, you'll be able to discover new and better marketing techniques before your competitors catch on. You can get in on the ground flow of new marketing platforms while they are uncrowded and therefore at maximum strength.

The Bulseye Framework will give you an inner circle of three traction channels, one of which you will choose to focus on. Keep doing that but also run some cheap tests in the other traction channels in your inner circle. These tests should determine what it costs you to acquire customers through that channel and what kind of business you do with them. Always keep looking for better, cheaper and more effective scalable growth. Run some A/B tests which allow you to understand the effectiveness of all your traction efforts. This will always be a moving target.

5. ALWAYS HAVE A TRACTION GOAL THAT MOVES THE NEEDLE

It's very easy for startups to get pulled in lots of different directions. You have to decide whether to work on product revisions, building the organization or whatever else comes along. With that in mind, you should always have a traction goal you're working on – and this needs to be something which will move the needle for your startup in a meaningful way.

Traction Goal

Critical Path

- Milestone 1
- Milestone 2
- Milestone 3
- Milestone 4
- Milestone 5

Remember, generating traction should take up 50% of your time so here's how to achieve good traction goals:

1. *Set a specific and meaningful traction goal* – maybe to get 1,000 new customers, 100 new users each day or 1% of your market. Set a challenging goal which will change your startup's prospects for the better when you achieve it.
2. *Identify your critical path to achieving that goal* – the milestones you will need to achieve in order to reach your goal. Order your milestones by which needs to be done first, second and so on. That sequence then sets out your critical path.
3. *Start assessing everything you do by that critical path* – does it move you forward or backward on that path? Teach all your employees that critical path and get them working on it as well.
4. *Get some mentors* – who will be able to teach you how to move down your critical path more effectively.

5. *Be aware of your biases* – you will naturally prefer one traction channel over another. Work to overcome those biases by enlisting the help of your mentors and by taking a data-based approach. Use data to determine which traction channels are working the best and stick with them.

THE NINETEEN TRACTION CHANNELS

CHANNEL # 1 VIRAL MARKETING: GET EXISTING USERS TO REFER OTHER NEW USERS

For a startup, going viral means each new user you acquire brings in one or more other users and the cycle repeats. This can create impressive exponential growth – as exemplified by the rise of Facebook, Twitter, WhatsApp and others.

In practice, viral growth is hard to achieve. You need a perfect storm of different factors to come together for it to happen. More realistically, you should try and get a simple viral loop working along these lines:

1. A new customer is exposed to your product and likes what you offer
2. That customer is incentivized to tell his or her friends and associates
3. Those potential users are exposed to your product and become users

You track both your viral coefficient (the number of additional users you get for each new user) and your viral cycle time and then progressively try new things. If you can get your viral coefficient to 0.5, that's still strong growth. A viral coefficient over 1.0 means you're generating exponential growth.

You then keep testing different combinations of elements to try and boost your viral coefficient and reduce your cycle time. Sometimes it's also smart to copy someone else's viral loop until your own kicks in. The great characteristic of a robust viral loop is once you get one working, it becomes self-sustaining. Do all you can to add a bunch of viral features and build on any pockets which emerge. Test everything and identify exactly what works. Then figure out a way to give users more of that.

CHANNEL # 2 PUBLIC RELATIONS: GET YOUR NAME OUT THERE USING TRADITIONAL MEDIA

Public relations or PR is all about getting news outlets, newspapers and magazines to write about what you're doing. If you can get free coverage, that can lead to a large volume of new customers and traction.

The dirty little secret of the publishing industry is the big players steal ideas from the small players all the time. That means to get on CNN or in *The Wall Street Journal*, you don't have to pitch them directly. Instead, get a small local publication involved and then amplify that to the bigger players. This is called "filtering up."

Of course, tens of thousands of companies are trying to do the same thing so a little bit of creativity is required. To make the most of your PR opportunities:

- Be genuinely newsworthy.
- Build relationships with reporters who cover your startup's target market niche. Read what they report and offer your expertise as a market commentator should they want it.
- Package your news stories around genuinely news-worthy milestones or compelling emotional stories (which just happen to feature your product in a favorable light.)
- Figure out the messaging and brand positioning you want to project and then unify your messages around those themes.
- Stay on trend. Understand what's happening in your market and what a genuine breakthrough looks like. Pick an angle that works and stay with it.
- Whenever you do make a pitch, keep it short and sweet. Reporters will love that.
- If you are fortunate enough to get a story published, tell the world. Submit it to community sites with larger audiences. Share it on your social networks. Email it to influencers in your industry and to major publications. Make sure everyone knows about it.

Unconventional public relations comes in two types:

Unconventional PR

- *Publicity stunts* – where you do something outrageous to attract media attention
- *Customer appreciation* – you make small gestures which turn customers into evangelists

The gold standard for publicity stunts is Richard Branson who has done some pretty outlandish things. By creating a spectacle, Branson transforms ordinary product launches into national headlines. The right kind of publicity stunt can generate instant recognition for you.

Customer appreciation is much more scalable and consistent. In practice, this involves finding practical ways to tell customers "you're awesome!" You might give them gifts, run contests or offer exceptional customer services. These are all tangible and sustainable forms of customer appreciation. Another great way to show customer appreciation is to showcase your best customers to the press.

Admittedly, success in this channel is unpredictable. Not every idea you come up with will work. That's par for the course whenever and wherever you take risks. But again, if you get this right, the results can be awe-inspiring. For example, when new search engine company DuckDuck-Go bought a billboard outside Google's headquarters trumpeting it's privacy focus, it lead to national press stories in *USA Today, Wired* and others. Going up against the top dog in your field can be a great way to generate some unconventional PR. DuckDuckGo managed to more than double its user base by being audacious enough to challenge the biggest player that exists.

CHANNEL # 4 SEARCH ENGINE MARKETING: PAY TO HAVE YOUR ADS SHOW UP IN RESULTS

Advertisers spend more than $100 million a day on Google's AdWords platform. Why? Because it works. You can jump on the bandwagon by using pay-per-click (PPC) advertising which links your ads to keywords being used in online searches.

The key PPC parameters are:

- Your click-through rate – the percentage of ad impressions which result in clicks.
- Cost-per-click – which is how much you have to pay for each click on your ad.
- Cost-per-acquisition – how much you pay to acquire a new customer.

The good thing about search engine marketing is you can use it to test product positioning, features and messaging even before you fully build your product. If you get something which resonates with the marketplace as proven by your search results, that's surely a good indicator of future success.

It's probably helpful to have realistic expectations about search engine marketing. Your first ads are unlikely to be profitable while you test keywords, ad copy, landing pages, product elements, etc. If you run an ad campaign that gets close to breakeven, that might indicate search engine marketing is viable and worth using. Keep testing these elements against profitability.

> "We suggest everyone run some SEM tests because they are straightforward, cheap to do and can give you insights into your business."
>
> *- Gabriel Weinberg and Justin Mares*

> "SEM works well for companies looking to sell directly to their target customer. You are capturing people that are actively searching for solutions. The scale of search engines is so vast that this channel works for any product phase."
>
> *- Gabriel Weinberg and Justin Mares*

CHANNEL # 5 SOCIAL/DISPLAY ADS: ADVERTISE ON POPULAR SITES LIKE YOUTUBE, FACEBOOK

Large brands pay millions each year to place banner ads on popular websites and on social sites. These ads can be placed by networks like Google's Display Network or by the advertiser themselves.

Banner ads are display ads which appear electronically as opposed to being in print. They allow you to reach a broad audience and typically have embedded links so the viewer can take immediate action. You will have to pay to be on a well-known website but you can also contact smaller sites directly and ask them to run your ads. In these cases, it's not unusual for the fee they ask for to be very modest.

Banner ads really harvest demand – you link to people who are actively searching for something right now. By contrast, advertising on social media sites tends to be more about demand generation. On social sites, you engage with people and gradually build an audience over time. Social media ads engage people and gradually convert them into customers.

The key to successful display ads and social ads is to create compelling content and engaging experiences. Study what your competitors are doing and test their approaches for yourself. As you run A/B tests on your ads, you will get to understand your target audience better and figure out memorable ways to appeal to them.

The best social and display ads usually go hand-in-hand with content marketing. Getting people interested enough to give you their contact details in exchange for alluring content is a widely used marketing strategy. You can then follow up and re-engage them over and over. Social and display ads are great ways to start conversations with prospective customers.

Just keep in mind users are visiting social media to be entertained or to interact with others, not to be sold something. Effective ads will encourage that to happen without being intrusive or pushy. That's a nice balance to achieve.

CHANNEL # 6 OFFLINE ADS: PAY FOR TV SPOTS, RADIO COMMERCIALS, FLYERS, ETC.

Offline ads have been used by businesses to build a customer base for eons. Even today, advertisers spend more on offline ads than they do on online advertising. Offline ads are cheap, easy to test and enormously flexible in the way they can be used.

The variety of offline ads is impressive and includes TV, radio, newspapers, magazines, yellow pages, billboards, direct mail and more. Each of these will have a target audience attached so that means you can select the vehicle which is most likely to appeal to your target customer demographic.

Some suggestions for using offline ads to best effect would include:

- *Always inquire about remnant ad inventory* – ad space that is currently unused and therefore likely to be available at a substantial discount off the rate card. This can be a great way to run some cheap tests before you commit to spending more.
- *Build tracking into your ad* – by having customers go to a specific URL or use a unique promotional code in their order. You need to figure out what's working and what is not.
- *Start local* – and then scale up to regional or national if the demand and the results you achieve warrants it. This applies not only to print ads but also to TV ads. There are more than 1,300 local TV stations in the United States alone and their advertising rate cards are often reasonably priced. If your ads pull well in local markets, you can then look at harnessing the networks to amplify your results.

Before the Internet came along, most large companies got their starts by using offline advertising and it still works well today. Just keep reminding yourself you can't forecast in advance what will work and what will not. You just have to keep trying different types of advertising until you find something which generates some decent traction for your enterprise.

CHANNEL # 7 SEARCH OPTIMIZATION: MAKE SURE YOUR WEBSITE SHOWS UP IN SEARCHES

Search engine optimization or SEO is the process of getting your website to rank highly in the results online search engines show. In practice, most people will tend to only click on the first ten results which are shown so the higher your ranking on search engines, the better.

SEO tactics come in two flavors:

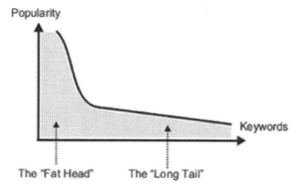

- If you're going for the fat-head of the demand curve, you try to link in with short and obvious keywords. You then embed quality content and numerous links into your online material so you rank highly.

- The other alternative is to employ a long-tail approach. Here you tie in with long and highly specific keywords which attract less searches individually but in the aggregate make up more than 70% of all searches.

As a general rule-of-thumb, most startups tend to focus on a bundle of long-tail keywords to start building traction and then gradually migrate to more of a fat-head approach later on. Both approaches really require quality content and numerous links to be sustainable. If you're producing amazing content, search optimization is the perfect way to let future customers find you.

CHANNEL # 8 CONTENT MARKETING: USE YOUR BLOG TO GENERATE NEW CUSTOMERS

Content marketing is where you post quality content on your blog and that attracts comments, social media shares, leads and ultimately new customers. The good thing about this traction channel is the content you post on your blog can also enhance the results you get from search engines, PR, email marketing, offline events and so on. When you get good content marketing happening, it can generate lots of new customers.

This is not as simple as posting good content on your blog and then siting back. Lots of companies have blogs which are infrequently updated, attract few if any comments and frankly are pretty boring and unproductive. To avoid that fate, you might try to use ideas which have worked for others:

- Start your blog as a marketing vehicle while you're still in your product development phase. Detail what you're doing and get your future customers engaged. An interesting blog-from-the-beginning like this can generate a pool of people who are anxious for you to launch.
- Use your blog as the focal point for all your marketing activities. Post controversial material there and let people comment. Write about solutions to the problems your target customers face in entertaining and slightly controversial ways and you will often attract lots of attention.
- Don't forget to mix it up – include mini-courses, ebooks and infographics in your posts. Or maybe offer these goodies for their email address.
- Find the online forums where your target customers already are and contribute. Point back to your blog with each post you make in those forums.
- Get interesting guests to post on your blog.

The great thing about using a blog to generate traction is it automatically positions you as a leader in your space. That can lead to opportunities to speak in conferences and to be quoted in other publications.

CHANNEL # 9 EMAIL MARKETING: USE EMAIL TO CONVERT PROSPECTS AND SELL

Email is still the main workhorse of the online world. It can be used to deliver coupons, referrals, sales pitches and more. You can use it to find future customers, engage your present customers, retain more customers and more. Email works because it's personalized and therefore relevant.

For all the potential complexity that exists, success in using email to generate traction generally comes down to two basic building blocks:

Email

- *Your mailing list* – people who have given you their contact details to keep in touch
- *Automated responders*– which send out a sequence of email messages over a set period
- You keep a mailing list of potential customers and send them more material in the future to fan that spark of interest and turn it into a purchase transaction.
- You set up an automated series of emails which takes people through your sales funnel. This life-cycle or drip sequence happens automatically in the background as good quality material is sent.

One of email's enduring strengths is the fact the recipient can talk back to you via email. You can find out about problems, suggestions, support needs, feature requests and more via what people say in their email. You can use that information to figure out how to sell more people in the future.

> *"If you're running a real business, [email] is still the most effective way to universally reach people who have expressed interest in your product or site. For that, it really can't be beat."*
>
> *- Colin Nederkoorn, founder, Customer.io*

CHANNEL # 10 ENGINEERING AS MARKETING: GIVE AWAY FREE TOOLS WHICH GENERATE LEADS

A great way to generate traction is to get your engineering team to build some tools and resources people need. You then give away those tools to get your company in front of potential customers. When done well, this can generate a torrent of leads.

So how does this work? Take a few examples:

- Hubspot is a marketing automation software company. It offers a free Website Grader which generates a customized report about how well you're doing with your online marketing. This free tool generates more than 50,000+ qualified leads per month for Hubspot. More than three million sites have been through the Website Grader.
- WPEngine, a hosting company, offers a free tool which checks how fast a WordPress site loads. It asks for an

email address for the report to be sent to and that sets off an automated sequence offering a free mini-course and other goodies.

- Codecademy offered a free coding lesson each week for a year at the beginning of 2012. More than 450,000 individuals signed up – nearly doubling Codecademy's user base at that time.
- Delicious developed a widget (a tool that is embeddable on other sites) which more than tripled their user base.
- Analytics company RJMetrics used their own product and then posted the results on the most popular social media sites. Readers were attracted by that material and some became customers.
- Search engine company DuckDuckGo set up a dedicated micro-site in 2011 which showed how Google tracks your searches and how that might harm you. This not only raised awareness of DuckDuckGo's main point of differentiation but it also continues to generate leads. DuckDuckGo now has four micro-sites set up and feeding traffic to the main business website.

CHANNEL # 11 TARGETING BLOGS: CREATE AWARENESS THROUGH BLOG POSTS

Posting material on other people's blogs is an effective way to start generating traction. The only problem this is not really scalable. There will generally be an upper limit on the number of blogs which are relevant. Still, this is sometimes a good way to start the ball rolling and get your first wave of customers.

The best tools for finding blogs which will be relevant to you are:

- YouTube
- Delicious
- StumbleUpon
- Twitter
- Google Alerts
- All the main search engines

It usually makes sense to start small and work your way up to the major leagues. Run some tests on some small blogs and see what kind of audience responds best to what you offer. Once you get your messages fine-tuned on those small blogs, you can then start targeting the big blogs with millions of followers.

Another great way to use other people's blogs to build your own momentum is to look for small blog sponsor-ship opportunities. Personal blogs often won't ask for much and this can be effective. If you also offer influential bloggers early access to your future releases in exchange for spreading the word, that can appeal to them as well.

Closely aligned to using other people's blogs is to use the many link-sharing communities which exist on the Internet. When Dropbox was in startup mode, it posted a video on Hacker News which attracted more than 10,000 sign-ups. That was enough to get Dropbox trending on Digg – which in turn attracted another wave of sign-ups. This is a great way to seed your own traction efforts. Link sharing can generate buzz, feedback and traffic when done right.

CHANNEL # 12 BUSINESS DEVELOPMENT: CREATE USEFUL STRATEGIC RELATIONSHIPS

With sales, you're selling directly to a customer. Business development means you partner with someone else and then work together to reach customers in ways which will benefit both parties.

Business development partnerships can be structured in lots of different ways:

- *Standard partnerships* – where you and another company agree to work together to develop and then sell your own products.
- *Joint ventures* – where you work with partners to create entirely new product offerings.
- *Licensing* – where a startup uses another company's customer base and pays them a royalty on all sales which result.
- *Distribution deals* – where you agree to sell someone else's product or vice versa.
- *Supply partnerships* – you secure exclusive or restricted access to key inputs for certain products.

Business development initiatives like these can generate some significant traction for a startup. As long as you pick the right partner and align with forward thinkers, deals and alliances like these can deliver some appealing benefits.

The stark reality, however, is many business development deals fail despite the best efforts of everyone involved. Rather than looking at this as a one-off initiative, the smart approach is to create a pipeline of potential deals. Reach out to a variety of potential partners and do some cheap tests and see what emerges.

> *"There's no reason why any company shouldn't have 50 potential business development partners in their pipeline, maybe 100, and be actively working the phones, inboxes, and pounding the pavement to get the deals you need to get."*
>
> *- Charlie O'Donnell, Brooklyn Bridge Ventures*

CHANNEL # 13 SALES: CREATE SCALABLE DIRECT SALES PROCESSES

Obviously when you generate leads, qualify them and then convert them into customers, that gives you traction. The challenge is how to scale this traction channel effectively.

Ideally you want your first customers to give glowing reviews of what you've done for them so as to generate buzz. That means you need to identify prospects who have a burning need for what you offer. You will then want to work closely with them to validate the solution does what they need. This is more likely to happen for high-ticket items than for low-priced mass market products.

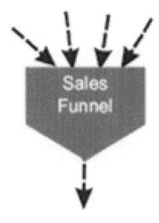

The underlying goal of sales for any startup is to come up with a repeatable and effective sales funnel. You need to build processes which generate an ongoing stream of qualified leads. Within the sales funnel, those prospects then need to be closed or put into programs which nurture them for future sales.

The best sales funnels tend to be designed from the standpoint of the customer rather than the company. If you can put in place systems which reduce the complexity of the buying process while at the same time amplifying the benefits which accrue, then you can build more and more traction.

Early sales can be highly motivational as well. If you attract quality first customers, you can build a sales funnel which will appeal to their peers. That's ideal for generating more traction.

CHANNEL # 14 AFFILIATE PROGRAMS: OFFER A COMMISSION ON NEW BUSINESS

Affiliate programs are where you pay people or companies for performing specified actions or achieving specific results. They are commonly used in retail, information products and broader lead generation programs:

- Retail: Amazon, Target and Wal-Mart pay between 4% and 8.5% of each sale to any affiliate which refers them. Coupons, daily deals and loyalty programs are variations on the affiliate theme and are widely used.
- Information products: Clickbank has more than 100,000 affiliates who receive commissions on sales of millions of digital products every year.
- Lead generation: Some insurance companies pay a commission of $50 to $100 for every lead they receive. Lead generation is a $26 billion industry so this is very

well established practice.

To use an affiliate program to generate traction for your startup, evaluate how passionate your initial customers are. There are lots of online services you can use to track the results of what your affiliates generate for you so tracking is pretty straightforward. Usually the hardest part of setting up an affiliate program is to figure out how much to pay your affiliates.

You've got to pay affiliates enough to motivate them and do this in a sustainable way for your business. Some companies pay their affiliates a flat fee for every sale whereas others pay a percentage of any sales which result. It's also common to have tiers built in so high-performing affiliates earn more. Sometimes you will also be able to pay your affiliates with more of your product rather than in cash.

Don't forget you also need to provide affiliates with the tools they will need to succeed as well. Building those tools and making them widely available will enhance the traction you generate through affiliates. This is a very useful channel for a startup to use.

CHANNEL # 15 EXISTING PLATFORMS: USE FACEBOOK, APP STORE TO GENERATE LEADS

Platforms like the Android and Apple app stores have hundreds of millions of users. The major social media platforms (such as Facebook, Twitter and Pintrest) number billions of users worldwide. If you can get a top ranking app or a major story covered on these platforms, you have the potential to reach millions of users in days or months rather than years or decades.

Breaking into the top rankings or getting a major story covered just might set off a self-sustaining loop which snowballs and attracts even more attention in the future. Admittedly, achieving this is pretty tough for all the major platforms as everyone is trying to do the same thing.

So how can you increase your chances of success? There are a few things you can try:

1. Figure out where your potential customers tend to hang out online and identify what it will take to stand out in that niche.
2. Focus on one platform at a time and come up with something compellingly good for your potential customers. Do whatever it takes to be highly ranked or featured on that platform.
3. See if you can identify any gaps in the features which the platform itself offers. Large companies have been built in the past just by providing features which the platform was not delivering. Add-ons and extensions are a savvy way to gain traction.
4. Keep a keen eye out for emerging platforms which you may be able to coattail on. There's less competition to be doing things for those platforms and if they gain traction, you go along for the ride. Admittedly this

strategy also means if the platform stalls, your opportunities for growth go away as well but if you get it right, you can enjoy incredible growth.

Piggybacking on the explosive growth of an emerging or an established platform is a widely used traction strategy. See if it's an option for you.

CHANNEL # 16 TRADE SHOWS: SHOW OFF LATEST PRODUCTS AND SELL DIRECTLY

Trade shows provide an opportunity to interact with customers, partners and the press within a few short days. Used well, being at the right trade show at the right time can generate a turbo boost of traction.

Ideally, you should attend a trade show the year before you participate and figure out the lay of the land. You can talk to those who are exhibiting and make sure you understand who comes along. Armed with that knowledge, you can then set some realistic traction goals for the following year's edition of that trade show.

You will need both an inbound and an outbound strategy for your booth at a trade show:

1. *Inbound strategy* – You structure your booth around what you're trying to achieve by being there – land some major customers, get press coverage, form some significant alliances, etc. You also figure out what you'll do to attract a crowd and generate buzz _ giveaways, promotions, particularly engaging displays, etc.

2. *Outbound strategy* _ You also figure out what you need to be doing away from the trade show floor. This might be taking people to dinner or going to social settings where you can get introduced to key industry players in a casual setting. Or you might throw a party near the trade show and invite all the movers and shakers to come along.

As with any other traction channel, utilizing a trade show is a matter of figuring out how to get the most bang for your buck. You also have to fit the trade show into your operating budget. Preparation is the secret sauce for success at trade shows.

> *"This is one of the few times during the year when nearly everyone in your industry is in one place; you'll want to be at your best. Your preparation for a trade show will determine how successful you will be."*
>
> *- Gabriel Weinberg and Justin Mares*

CHANNEL # 17 OFFLINE EVENTS: SPONSOR OR RUN CONFER-ENCES OR EVENTS

Sponsoring or putting together offline events can be a superb way to get traction. Companies like Apple, Oracle and Salesforce have done this for years. Importantly, conferences are particularly useful for startups which have long sales cycles. You can use them to build relationships and to signal what's coming soon.

Events covers a wide range of options right across the spectrum:

- You can run an industry-wide conference featuring all the leading thought makers in your field.
- You might set up a one-day mini conference. Eric Ries launched the lean startup movement by running a one-day mini conference in San Francisco titled "Startup Lessons Learned."
- Instead of a major conference, a better way to gain traction might be to run a meetup or a smaller scale event. You gather a small group of influencers and talk with them. You could even hold a meetup in different cities across the country. This is a great way to create grassroots connections.
- You might go all out and throw a party to gain traction. Companies like Evian and Yelp have used this strategy with impressive success.

"I think the overarching thing for marketing is start-ups need to try more things, and fail faster and more quickly. The tried and true approaches like Facebook and AdWords are so crowded now. People need to think about doing things that don't scale. You can still build a business without being creative. If you don't have creativity, you need money. You need one or the other."

- Rob Walling, founder of MicroConf

CHANNEL # 18 SPEAKING ENGAGEMENTS: GIVE ADDRESSES WHICH CREATE BUZZ

This is a relatively easy traction channel to start with. You offer to give free talks to small groups and work your way up. As you talk to small groups, you'll find you fine-tune your message and increase in confidence which will stand you in good stead to move to the next level.

The real key to landing speaking engagements is to become an expert in your field. Whenever you see an event come along which is a good match with your expertise, you contact the event organizers and make them aware of your credentials and your availability. In this way, you leverage what you do at small groups to gain invitations to participate in large scale events.

Delivering a memorable public address is usually a matter of being able to tell an engaging story and then helping people draw the right conclusions from what you say. All great public speakers are storytellers first and foremost.

Slides and visuals also bring your ideas to life. Try and develop a simple set of visuals with each one being about a 7 minute story with its own beginning, middle and end. If you're then asked to give a 60 minute presentation, you just add more slides. Alternatively, if you only have 20 minutes, you can take slides out.

It's also smart to leverage your talks on social media. If possible, have someone record you in action and post clips on YouTube. Or you might ask the audience to tweet you if they identify with a point you're making. You can then go back and fine-tune which parts of your speech have the most impact. You can also use social media effectively to deliver your call-to-action at the conclusion of your speech.

The more public speeches you give, the better you will get at this and the more traction you will enjoy.

CHANNEL # 19 COMMUNITY BUILDING: CREATE GROUPS OF PASSIONATE USERS

Pure and simple community building is all about creating evangelists for your startup. You get together a group of people and then have them spread the word about how awesome you are.

As with public speaking, you build a community by starting small. You get a small group of users together and grow from there. If everyone feels like they are on a mission, your community's sense of purpose and drive will attract more like-minded individuals.

The things you can do to increase the community building which happens might include:

• *Foster and facilitate cross-connections* – where users

connect with each other and do fun stuff.
- *Communicate with your community all the time* – give them the inside information they crave and value.
- *Always be transparent* – let them buy into your mission.
- *Focus on getting quality people into your community* – and have some processes which ensure ongoing quality.
- *Let your community help develop your products* – use their ideas for the direction you go with your product development. Leverage your community to achieve your mission.
- *Recruit and hire from your community* – look at this as the perfect breeding ground for future talent.

A vibrant user community has always been a great way to increase traction. Not only do you build a valuable asset but you create more evangelists whenever a community comes together around your products. When you go down this route, you're following in the footsteps of some highly successful companies. Go forth and generate traction.

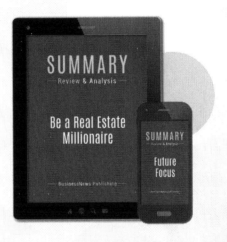